Presented to

_____

by_____

on_____

Is God Always with Me?

Crystal Bowman
Illustrated by Elena Kucharik

Tyndale House Publishers, Inc.
CAROL STREAM, ILLINOIS

Visit Tyndale's exciting Web site at www.tyndale.com

TYNDALE is a registered trademark of Tyndale House Publishers, Inc.
Tyndale Kids logo is a trademark of Tyndale House Publishers, Inc.

Little Blessings is a registered trademark of Tyndale House Publishers, Inc.
The Little Blessings characters are a trademark of Elena Kucharik.

Is God Always with Me?

Edited by Betty Free Swanberg
Designed by Catherine Bergstrom

Scripture quotations are taken from the *Holy Bible,* New Living Translation, copyright © 1996,
2004. Used by permission of Tyndale House Publishers, Inc., Carol Stream, Illinois 60188.
All rights reserved.

Library of Congress Cataloging-in-Publication Data

Bowman, Crystal.
      Is God always with me? / Crystal Bowman; illustrated by Elena Kucharik.
            p. cm. — (Little blessings)
      ISBN-13: 978-1-4143-0287-4 (alk. paper)
      ISBN-10: 1-4143-0287-8 (alk. paper)
      1. Presence of God—Juvenile literature. 2. Presence of God—Biblical teaching. I. Kucharik, Elena.
II. Title. III. Little blessings picture books.
      BT180.P6B69 2005
      231.7—dc22   2004024176

Printed in Singapore

11   10   09   08   07   06
6   5   4   3

The LORD keeps watch over you as you come and go,
both now and forever.
Psalm 121:8

Is God always with me
wherever I go?
Is he with me each minute?
I'd sure like to know!

Can God always hear me

wherever I pray?

Can I talk to God

any time of the day?

If Kaitlyn's afraid

when the thunder goes *BOOM!*

Is God close beside her

right there in her room?

Zoë looks sad

when her friend says good-bye.

What will God do

if they both start to cry?

When Jack is sick

with a cold or the flu,

Will God make him better?

What can *I* do?

When Zoë needs help

because she is small,

Will God help her out

if she gives him a call?

What if I'm bad

and I do not obey?

Will God be upset?

Will he go far away?

When it's my birthday,

is God there to see

The big birthday cake

that was made just for me?

16

The Bible tells us
    as plain as can be
That God is with you
    and God is with me.

At school or at home,
    in a bus or a car,
God's always with you
    wherever you are.

Before you were born,

    God was waiting for you.

And now that you're here,

    God is here with you too.

God knows when you eat,

and he watches you play.

He sees when you sleep

at the end of the day.

Whenever you need him,

God will be there.

He's happy to listen

to every prayer.

You can pray any time

of the day or the night.

At home or away,

any place is just right.

God is with Kaitlyn

and he is with you

Through thunder and rain

and quiet times too.

So don't be afraid,

'cause you're never alone.

God is right there

in your very own home.

Zoë is sad

that her friend went away,

But God's with them both

wherever they stay.

God cares about you

if you're sad or upset.

He sends you his love—

it's the best you can get!

If your friend's sick in bed,

God will be there.

Just pray for your friend.

God will answer your prayer.

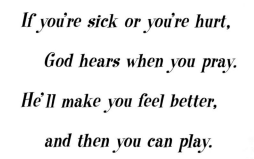

If you're sick or you're hurt,

God hears when you pray.

He'll make you feel better,

and then you can play.

36

Riding a bike

or tying your shoe—

Sometimes these things

can be hard to do.

But God's here to help you,

so maybe he'll send

A parent who cares,

or a neighbor or friend.

It makes God sad

when you disobey.

But God still loves you—

he won't go away.

Tell God you're sorry
when you have been bad.
Then God will forgive you,
and you will be glad.

God's there on your birthday

and all through the year.

Each day of the week

God will always be near.

He helps you to learn,

and he helps you to grow.

He shows you the way

that he wants you to go.

God says that he's with you

each day and each night,

And you can believe him

'cause God's always right!

You know God is with you,

so put on a smile.

He'll be with you forever,

and that's a long while!

Bible References

The answers in this poem come from God's Word. Talking about these Bible verses with your child will help your little one understand that the Bible answers all of our questions about whether God is always with us. You may want to open your Bible and show your child where these verses can be found.

The Bible tells us as plain as can be
That God is with you and God is with me.
At school or at home, in a bus or a car,
God's always with you wherever you are.

The LORD your God is with you wherever you go. JOSHUA 1:9

You see me when I travel and when I rest at home. PSALM 139:3

[Jesus said,] "Be sure of this: I am with you always." MATTHEW 28:20

Before you were born, God was waiting for you.
And now that you're here, God is here with you too.
God knows when you eat, and he watches you play.
He sees when you sleep at the end of the day.

You saw me before I was born. Every day of my life was recorded in your book. PSALM 139:16

You go before me and follow me. . . . I can never escape from your Spirit! I can never get away from your presence! PSALM 139:5, 7

Whenever you need him, God will be there.
He's happy to listen to every prayer.
You can pray any time of the day or the night.
At home or away, any place is just right.

> Never stop praying. 1 Thessalonians 5:17

> We are confident that he hears us whenever we ask for anything that pleases him. And since we know he hears us when we make our requests, we also know that he will give us what we ask for. 1 JOHN 5:14-15

God is with Kaitlyn and he is with you
Through thunder and rain and quiet times too.
So don't be afraid, 'cause you're never alone.
God is right there in your very own home.

> I know the LORD is always with me. I will not be shaken, for he is right beside me. PSALM 16:8

> He calmed the storm to a whisper. PSALM 107:29

> Do not be afraid, for I am with you. ISAIAH 43:5

Zoë is sad that her friend went away,
But God's with them both wherever they stay.
God cares about you if you're sad or upset.
He sends you his love—it's the best you can get!

> Don't be . . . sad, for the joy of the LORD is your strength! NEHEMIAH 8:10

> Give all your worries and cares to God, for he cares about you. 1 PETER 5:7

If your friend's sick in bed, God will be there.
Just pray for your friend. God will answer your prayer.
If you're sick or you're hurt, God hears when you pray.
He'll make you feel better, and then you can play.

[Jesus] healed every kind of disease and illness. MATTHEW 9:35

A prayer offered in faith will heal the sick, and the Lord will make you well. JAMES 5:15

Riding a bike or tying your shoe—
Sometimes these things can be hard to do.
But God's here to help you, so maybe he'll send
A parent who cares, or a neighbor or friend.

God is our refuge and strength, always ready to help in times of trouble. PSALM 46:1

My help comes from the LORD, who made heaven and earth! PSALM 121:2

As soon as I pray, you answer me; you encourage me by giving me strength. PSALM 138:3

It makes God sad when you disobey.
But God still loves you—he won't go away.
Tell God you're sorry when you have been bad.
Then God will forgive you, and you will be glad.

The LORD your God . . . will neither fail you nor abandon you. DEUTERONOMY 31:6

Give thanks to the LORD, for he is good! His faithful love endures forever. PSALM 118:1

If we confess our sins to him, he is faithful and just to forgive us our sins and to cleanse us from all wickedness. 1 John 1:9

God's there on your birthday and all through the year.
Each day of the week God will always be near.
He helps you to learn, and he helps you to grow.
He shows you the way that he wants you to go.

> You will show me the way of life, granting me the joy of your presence and the pleasures of living with you forever. PSALM 16:11

> The LORD directs the steps of the godly. He delights in every detail of their lives. PSALM 37:23

God says that he's with you each day and each night,
And you can believe him 'cause God's always right!
You know God is with you, so put on a smile.
He'll be with you forever, and that's a long while!

> I lay down and slept, yet I woke up in safety, for the LORD was watching over me. PSALM 3:5

> The LORD keeps watch over you as you come and go, both now and forever. PSALM 121:8

About the Author

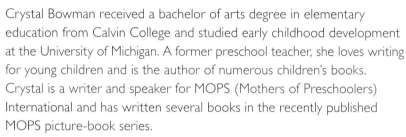

Crystal Bowman received a bachelor of arts degree in elementary education from Calvin College and studied early childhood development at the University of Michigan. A former preschool teacher, she loves writing for young children and is the author of numerous children's books. Crystal is a writer and speaker for MOPS (Mothers of Preschoolers) International and has written several books in the recently published MOPS picture-book series.

Besides writing books, Crystal enjoys being active in the local schools, speaking at authors' assemblies, and conducting poetry workshops. Her books of humorous poetry are favorites in the classroom as well as at literacy conferences.

Crystal also serves in women's ministries, writes Bible study materials for her church, and speaks at women's conferences. She has been a guest on many Christian radio programs and has written a book of meditations for moms.

Crystal and her husband live in Grand Rapids, Michigan, and have three grown children.

About the Illustrator

Elena Kucharik, well-known Care Bears artist, has created the Little Blessings characters that appear in the line of Little Blessings products for young children and their families.

Born in Cleveland, Ohio, Elena received a bachelor of fine arts degree in commercial art at Kent State University. After graduation she worked as a greeting card artist and art director at American Greetings Corporation in Cleveland.

For more than 25 years Elena has been a freelance illustrator. During this time she was the lead artist and developer of Care Bears, as well as a designer and illustrator for major corporations and publishers. For over 10 years Elena has been focusing her talents on illustrations for children's books.

Elena and her husband live in Madison, Connecticut, and have two grown daughters.

Books in the Little Blessings Line